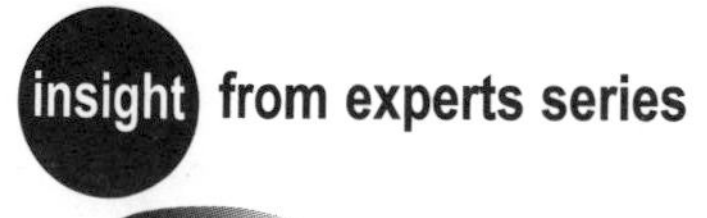

303 Solutions *for* Accomplishing More in Less Time

Compiled by
Doug Smart

James & Brookfield
J&B
Publishers

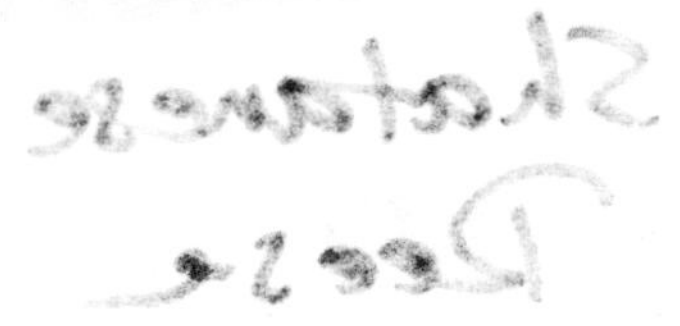

Managing Editor: Gayle Smart
Book Designer: Paula Chance

Disclaimer: This book is a compilation of ideas from numerous experts.
As such, the views expressed are those of the authors
and not necesasarily the views of James & Brookfield Publishers.

For more information, contact:
James & Brookfield Publishers
P.O. Box 768024
Roswell, GA 30076
770-587-9784

ISBN 0-9712851-6-0
Library of Congress Cataloging in Publication Data
10 9 8 7 6 5 4 3 2 1

"Dost thou love life?
Then do not squander time,
for that is the stuff
life is made of."

— Benjamin Franklin

1. **Seize the time.** The gift of life is an equal opportunity as no one gets more than 24 hours a day. Make them count.

— *John Storm*

2. **There is always time to do what is really important to you.** The difficult part is in deciding what is important.

— *Edie Raether*

3. **Live with purpose.** Boost the impact of your actions by believing in what you are spending time on!

— *Jo Spurrier*

4. **Design an action plan for your life.** Most people spend more time planning vacations and grocery lists than they do on their lives — and then wonder why they aren't more successful. Develop a plan and stick to it.

— *Martha Lanier*

5. **Discourage interruptions.** According to W. Edwards Demming, "The average American worker has fifty interruptions a day, of which 70% have nothing to do with work."

— Donna Satchel

6. **When it comes to ending procrastination, motivation comes from just getting started.** So dig right in. The toughest part of any task is just getting started. It will snowball on you.

— Linda Edgecombe

7. **Any person who develops the skills to concretely set goals and break them down into achievable steps, will find that his goals are attainable, and will find himself progressively advancing toward his goal(s).**

— Joe Gandolfo

8. **Clutter is an open-air filing system.**

— Doug Smart

9. **Reduce distracting clutter!** We look at everything in our sight range about once every eight seconds. In addition to looking, our mind is surveying what we see to determine if there are any threats, work not done, challenges, etc. All of this activity takes up our time, energy and detracts from our focus on the task at hand.

— Mike Monahan

10. **Unclutter Rule 1:** ***If it's stored somewhere else, toss yours.***

— Pat Veal

11. **Unclutter Rule 2:** ***If you haven't used it in a year, toss it.***

— Pat Veal

12. **Carry a mini-recorder attached to your key ring.** When you have a brilliant idea or you need to remember something, press record.

— Patti Wood

13. **Learn to type** — one of the things my dad told all of his kids. I learned to type in high school and it paid my way through college. I worked as a factory production clerk for 3-1/2 years, 50 hours a week, while I carried a full load at college. I can still type 70 words a minute and that really pays off in these days of computers.

— Greg Maciolek

14. **At night before going off to sleep make a list of the good things from that day.** When bad things come to mind slowly let them go as you breathe out.

— Robert Alan Black

15. **If you don't have time to do the things you say you want to do, you are saying they are not important enough to you to make the time.**

— Vicki Anderson

16. **Stop worshipping the multi-tasking gods.** Multi-tasking just isn't all it's cracked up to be. Your personality might be such that it is better to focus intently on one activity and get it done right rather than struggling to perfect task juggling.

— Diana Grippo

17. **Plan your year.** List your goals for the year allowing plenty of stretch room by making them somewhat bigger than you think is possible to reach. Next, define each of them in great detail, make sure they are measurable, give them time frames and share them with positive and supportive people.

— Martha Lanier

18. **Reevaluate your plan.** At least once each quarter have a meeting with yourself to evaluate your plan, learn what is working and what isn't, and then be willing to make adjustments. If plans are evaluated and adjusted every several months, then there are no hidden surprises at the end of the year.

— Martha Lanier

19. **Review your plan.** At the end of each year take the time to review your goals for the current year and list which ones you did accomplish and which ones you did not. Next determine what worked and what didn't so you can make adjustments to your plan the following year.

— Martha Lanier

20. **Choose to be optimistic.** How you think is everything. Research indicates optimists accomplish more than pessimists, according to Dr. Martin Seligman, author of *Learned Optimism.*

— *Doug Smart*

21. **Clean up your act!** Spend a Saturday and clean off your desk. Clutter adds to your stress. Regard your desk as a workspace not a storage unit. A clean desk will give you a psychological lift.

— *Linda Edgecombe*

22. **When building a daily "to do" list, include only those tasks that need to be done by you and are important to your job.** Delegate or trash everything else.

— *Vicki Anderson*

23. **Keep your lists short.** Never allow any list you keep in front of you or carry around with you to be longer than 6 items. Once you have accomplished your latest 6, celebrate and take a break.

— Robert Alan Black

24. **Throw away your clock!** Creativity and breakthrough ideas, which can put you on the leading edge, cannot be time-bound and require incubation independent of a one-dimensional experience of time.

— Edie Raether

25. **You need not always dot i's and cross t's.** Some things don't need to be done perfectly, they just need to be done.

— Pat Veal

26. **Capitalize on waiting.** Life is full of waiting. Waiting in line, on the phone, and in traffic to name a few. Think ahead, expect waiting, relax, and find something to do. Update your 'to do' list, write a thank you note, listen to an inspiring audiotape. Find ways to use the time that are creative and productive.

— *John Storm*

27. **Plan a mental work-out.** Seeking ways to develop your mental skills is good. Implementing a strategy to discover, learn, practice and grow skills is even better. Doing this consistently over a period of time, continually working out these skills, will develop your abilities beyond what you may have thought possible.

— *Joe Gandolfo*

28. **Reduce *mind clutter*.** Our minds constantly recycle everything we want to remember. This is a stressful and unreliable process that also interferes with our ability to focus on the task at hand. Writing things down, using a reliable time and task management system, and developing a system for reminding ourselves of important obligations in a manner our brain trusts will reduce mind clutter.

— *Mike Monahan*

29. **Keep a hard copy notebook of everything you send by snail mail**. Label the columns sent to, what was sent, date sent, the way it was mailed, reason sent (or project), confirmed as arrived by name and date. Have pockets for each month to hold any receipts. You can also keep a similar file on your computer with any e-mail confirmations.

— *Patti Wood*

30. **Control your distractions by scheduling your interruptions.** Arrange a set period each day that your phone goes directly to voice mail and your e-mail alert is off. At the very least, answer at your convenience. Predetermine specific times during the day to answer voice mail and e-mail and let folks know to expect your response by the day's end, not in a few hours. You decide what and who receives your energy.

— Jo Spurrier

31. **Tear articles out of magazines for reading later** and put them in a folder that you always keep with you to read during periods of inactivity such as picking up the kids at practice, sitting in doctors' offices, traveling, etc. Throw articles away after reading or mark in the corner where they should be filed.

— Vicki Anderson

32. **If you want workers to be empowered and accountable, they must be owners of their jobs.** Remember, only those people who own their jobs will be accountable. Otherwise, it is someone else's responsibility. Make them on-the-job entrepreneurs.

— *Greg Maciolek*

33. **Surround yourself with "Can Do" people.** Keeping company with people who are always getting things accomplished can spur you in action. Their "non-excuses" attitude can get you motivated into doing more than you thought you could do.

— *Donna Satchell*

34. **To build consensus, work at truly knowing the people with whom you work.** Make it a goal to turn them into friends and help them whenever you can.

— *Robert Alan Black*

35. **Ask *when*?** every time you are given a deadline. Keep in mind,"As soon as possible" is not a time or date.

— *Vicki Anderson*

36. If you update your outgoing voicemail message with "Today is Monday . . ." **be sure to update it daily!** An out-of-date message serves to evoke a mixture of pity and superiority when the person on the other end of the line hears your outdated message.

— *Diana Grippo*

37. **If updating your outgoing voice mail message daily stresses you, don't do it!** Updating an outgoing message every day can be a detail that creates stress in some people and doesn't really accomplish anything.

— *Diana Grippo*

38. **The amount of time needed to complete a task expands to fit the time available.** Knowing this, if you want to accomplish more in less time. Give yourself less time for every task you want to accomplish.

— Linda Edgecombe

39. **Accept that what they believe they heard is probably not what you meant or thought you really said.** Help smooth things out before problems develop by asking for clarification and repeating what was said.

— Robert Alan Black

40. **Know your first, second, and third items to be completed each day — and don't deviate.** These 3 items are not optional. Your day is not finished until these items are crossed off the list. Before you know it, you will be organizing your work day to handle your top issues first.

— Jo Spurrier

41. **Do not over-commit.** Learn to say no to requests that you have no interest in doing, are ill-equipped to do, will require more time than you have to spare. Say "yes" to requests that you have the time to fulfill thus allowing you to make a valuable contribution.

— *Donna Satchell*

42. **Ditch the Lone Ranger and build a team.** Human beings were created to live in community with others and to interact with others. Invest in building solid relationships based on mutual respect, trust, and an acknowledgement of each person's unique gifts. You'll discover that you can accomplish much more as a team than as the Lone Ranger.

— *John Storm*

43. When you are in charge, don't *manage* meetings! **Guide, lead, and coordinate them instead.**

— Robert Alan Black

44. **Have single-focused meetings.** Any meeting that focuses on more than one thing rarely accomplishes much. Pick a purpose: Data gathering, problem-solving, decision-making, implementation, whatever, and then stick to that focus. Produce an agenda and follow it.

— Greg Maciolek

45. Tired of long meetings? **Hold more *stand up* meetings to help shorten the average length of meetings.**

— Robert Alan Black

46. **Set a personal deadline before the actual deadline.**

— Pat Veal

47. **Take some *pondering time* to think strategically.** I call this my *forest and trees* time. Take 15 minutes a day to think about your purpose and goals, what you are doing with your time and what isn't getting done. These 15 minutes can be the most effective time you spend each day, with life-enhancing ramifications.

— Mike Monahan

48. **Use e-mail and voice mail, and pagers with keyboards to send yourself reminders** and messages when you're out of the office.

— Patti Wood

49. **Self-discipline is key to accomplishing more.** This usually means making yourself do things that don't feel natural. But the longer we do these unnatural things, the more habitual they become. Keep at it.

— Linda Edgecombe

50. **When organizing, *need, want, wish* and *dream* are categories for deciding what to do next.** Ask yourself, "What will be the best use of the time I have?"

— Robert Alan Black

51. **Use only one time management system for everything in your life.**

— Vicki Anderson

52. **Don't be any more organized than you have to be.**

— Doug Smart

53. **Don't waste time talking about a problem to someone who can do absolutely nothing about it.**

— Diana Grippo

54. **Take out your personal garbage.** If emotions accumulate they are much like garbage — after a few days no one can stand to be in the vicinity! As you are going about your daily activities, in the background your mind is working on these emotional situations. This dual activity zaps your productivity.

— Jo Spurrier

55. **Take a Break.** All work and no play make Jack a burned-out wreck. Sometimes accomplishing more means stepping back from the task.

— John Storm

56. **Always carry blank business cards as well as your own.** If someone does not have a card with them you can give them a blank card to fill out and give you. You will look like a prepared professional.

— Patti Wood

57. **Beware of the *rabbit syndrome.*** Don't chase events that pop up during the day like an untrained bird-dog chases rabbits that dart across the trail.

— Edie Raether

58. **When training a new staff person, you have one week to imprint your organization's values, attitudes and culture.** Be very effective and efficient in those first five days.

— Linda Edgecombe

59. **Maximize your productive time.** Whether you are an early bird, a nighthawk or just work better after eating chili peppers, make the most of that time and work like you are a working machine.

— Pat Veal

60. **Give your ideas last when you are the boss.** If you want your staff to be problem-solvers, let them generate solutions to their problems. When you, as boss, offer a solution at a problem-solving meeting, the effect is to chill creativity. When people know that what they have to say matters, they will offer many solutions to the problem. Besides that, they get ownership to the solution, which is desirable, too.

— *Greg Maciolek*

61. **If you are a visual person you will file by pile because you live by the adage, "out of sight out of mind."** If this is true for you accept it. And at the same time work at lessening the number of piles and the heights of them.

— *Robert Alan Black*

62. What do you currently use to organize your time? List every method. What's working for you and what's not? Everyone has a system. **It's imperative that we use the systems that are working for us not against us.**

— Linda Edgecombe

63. **Always meet with an agenda and a purpose.** Meeting just to meet is useless and energy draining. Once completed, it may be discovered that a simple e-mail or conference call could have accomplished in 10 minutes what took three hours (including travel).

— Pat Veal

64. **Stay focused.** My research indicates we can expect a 4 to 1 improvement in efficiency and use of time when we can focus on a task exclusively as opposed to when we are trying to accomplish something while being distracted.

— Mike Monahan

65. **Embrace a system.** Create an organization system that works for you.

— John Storm

66. **Doing mundane tasks routinely frees up energies for creativity. Doing complex tasks routinely inhibits innovative thinking.**

— Edie Raether

67. **Developing stress management and relaxation techniques will allow you to combat the performance-reducing changes of a *fight* or *flight response*.** Medical researchers have discovered that a person with a relaxed body (minimal body tension and a calm and quiet mind) when exposed to what he or she perceives to be a stressful circumstance, showed increased levels of negative physiological changes. In three minutes or less, the individual's body tension increased and the mind raced.

— Joe Gandolfo

68. **Become accountable to someone on your accomplishments.** Find an accountability partner or team to check up on you and your progress.

— John Storm

69. **Plan ahead to use waiting time wisely.** This can be accomplished by always having a book or magazine to read or paper on which to write. Also, always have your cell phone and address book with you so you can make needed calls, if it is appropriate to do so.

— Donna Satchell

70. *Dread time* is dead time. **Reduce the amount of *dread time* by doing the least favorite activity first.**

— Pat Veal

71. **Being disorganized results in you accomplishing less.** Know the areas you need to improve upon. Whether it is messy closets, stacks of unfiled papers, or unbalanced check books, make the needed changes. It can save you time and money. Learn how to get organized by taking a seminar, reading a book or visiting the various websites on the subject.

— Donna Satchell

72. **Tear articles out of magazines that you want to keep for reference** and file them in subject files. Don't read them until you need information on that topic.

— Vicki Anderson

73. **Have tools at the ready.** Keep the things you use most often nearby. Pencils, pens, White-out™, and reference books should all be in arm's reach.

— Mike Monahan

74. **Successful athletes work with a coach to help them raise their level of accomplishment.** Hire a personal coach to be your confidant, supporter, and someone who can help you accomplish more. Often just having someone to listen and bounce ideas off of allows us to see a clearer picture of what it is we want to do, otherwise solutions remain undiscovered in our minds.

— Martha Lanier

75. **Put a specific time period for accepting calls on your answering message so that callers will know when to call you.**

— Robert Alan Black

76. **If you want others to respect your time, *you* must respect it.**

— Edie Raether

77. **We teach people how to treat us.** As people get you *figured out*, they will no longer give you any more respect than you give yourself. If you want people to respect your time, opinions, and leadership, you have to respect them first. At present, if they respect you but not enough, you need to increase the respect you demonstrate before they follow your lead.

— Doug Smart

78. **Discipline your interruptions.** When working on a critical project, limit the number of times you check e-mail and voicemail.

— John Storm

79. **The concept of open-door management can be a source of unproductive interruptions.** Yes, managers need to be available and good communication between manager and worker is essential. That should not be interpreted to mean that every time any worker has an idea, concern, suggestion or need to talk that they should be allowed to break the manager's concentration by running into the manager's office. Set office hours. Set priority rules. Make sure people know when to interrupt and when to write it down for later.

— *Mike Monahan*

80. **Control telephone interruptions.** Return non-urgent phone calls after you have completed important projects. If you are in the middle of a project, ask the caller if you may return the call.

— Donna Satchell

81. **Avoid spreading yourself too thin by doing too many things at once.** This comes back to being unable to say no and wanting to please everyone. Remember the next time someone asks a favor of you, there has to be a break from when the question is asked to when you answer it. This gives you a few moments to decide if you want to do it or not, thus minimizing guilt and resentment.

— Linda Edgecombe

82. You become more and more strategic in your thinking when you stop to **think about how the action you are considering taking will benefit your goals, mission, and purpose for doing what you do in the future.** Simply ask, "How will doing 'x' help me produce result 'y'?"

— *Robert Alan Black*

83. **Quiet and introverted people have great ideas, too — sometimes you have to ask them to open up.** Invite them to participate. Provide a safe environment to offer contrary views. Be sure that the team's *verbal abuser* is on a leash. *Verbal abusers* are recognized by their normal response to most things, "That is the dumbest idea I've ever heard" or "We've already tried it that way."

— *Greg Maciolek*

84. **Don't get on the *overwhelm bus*.** Approach projects with a logical progression of steps, beginning, as Dr. Stephen Covey advocates, with the end in mind.

— Diana Grippo

85. Just as lifting weights will make your body stronger, **practicing deep breathing and progressive muscle relaxation techniques over a period of time will make your mental capacity stronger.** You will experience two benefits:

    • Create a *reservoir of relaxation* that can be tapped into as needed.

    • Build skills to use whenever needed to combat any physical tension or mental stress.

— Joe Gandolfo

86. **Request an indirect reply or response**, such as, "If it is ok, don't call me."

— Vicki Anderson

87. **Share your biggest fears, insecurities, and perceived weaknesses with your staff and family.** The weight off of your shoulders will make you more streamlined in your thinking, which can make you more efficient.

— *Linda Edgecombe*

88. **Lighten up. It is possible to enjoy work and still be professional.**

— *Pat Veal*

89. **Time activate your tasks.** Instead of keeping a long list of tasks, decide when in the next week you are going to work on each task. Record that task on that date in your planner. Take in to consideration due dates, complexity, other obligations, and importance. Don't obligate yourself to do things on a day that has no available capacity unless you reprioritize the day.

— *Mike Monahan*

90. **Organize *walk about* lunch breaks.** The goal is to disconnect from the office and take a mental break; therefore, ask for silence or the very least, no shoptalk. As you fall into the rhythm of walking, focus your attention on nature, notice the clouds and trees. You will be amazed at how energized and rejuvenated you will feel to handle the remaining day.

— Jo Spurrier

91. **In your home keep extras of things you use often.** For example have a box of pens in every room. Have several sets of scissors where you will use them. Have an extra hairbrush and lint remover by the door. Keep a comb, a packet of aspirin and a fingernail file in your briefcase and glove compartment. Wherever you say to yourself, "I need . . . " put one in a nearby spot so you do not waste time finding or fetching things from other rooms.

— Patti Wood

92. **Set times of the day you need total freedom.** On your phone message mention that you are not available between such and such times and ask for one or two specific times you can return their call.

— Robert Alan Black

93. **Go to work everyday.** Your boss depends on you being there and so does the company. Don't let them down — another thing my dad taught me. There is nothing worse than a reputation that you are unreliable. Be there and work hard.

— Greg Maciolek

94. **Anticipate opportunity.** Save yourself a follow-up appointment by preparing a solid proposal on your first appointment. You don't have to use it, but it's there if the opportunity arises.

— John Storm

95. **Your natural curiosity and drive will help you accomplish more.** Don't wait for permission to do something you long to do. Perhaps you have become accustomed to thinking you have to be an expert, perhaps hold a certain degree, in order to move in a particular direction. If you want to write or make a movie, you don't need a school's permission. And you don't have to drop everything and dedicate your life to it. Just take a little step. Your desire is telling you something.

— Diana Grippo

96. **Negative thinking triggers your negative emotions:** anxiety, anger, fear, negativism, frustration and distrust. This then leads to a frantic mental state, reduced concentration, low confidence and increased tension. And this can lead to generating lower levels of performance.

— Joe Gandolfo

97. **Positive thinking triggers your positive emotions:** joy, fun, love, optimism, determination and enjoyment. This then leads to a calm mental state, increased concentration, greater confidence and relaxed muscles. And this can lead to generating higher levels of performance.

— Joe Gandolfo

98. **Create a "not-to-do" list.**

— Edie Raether

99. **You are not perfect!** If you lean towards the standard of perfection, you may become bogged down in details and find it difficult to vary your speed according to priorities. The solution is to purposely drop your standards a bit. Decide you will only go for 80% success on any given item as opposed to 100%.

— Linda Edgecombe

100. **Become a groupie.** Learn the art of grouping similar tasks for greater efficiency.

— John Storm

101. It's an old saying, but needs to be said again. **Handle paper once.** To bring this wisdom into the 21st century, add e-mail and voicemail. Deal with it, file it, or trash it. Don't let stuff linger on your desk or laptop. This keeps things from falling through the cracks.

— Linda Edgecombe

102. **E-mail mania.** Determine specific times to check your e-mail and turn off or lower the volume on your computer so you don't hear when new mail arrives. The time it takes our brains to shift our focus from our current project to checking for new e-mail can be the difference between leaving our desks on time and having to delay our departure by an hour or more.

— Martha Lanier

103. **Use e-mail for inquires that do not require a lengthy phone conversation.** If you only need a quick response to a question or idea, use e-mail. Many phone conversations require pleasantries that can be disruptive and unnecessary. Also e-mail can replace the game of "phone tag" which can be frustrating, time-consuming and nonproductive.

— Donna Satchell

104. **Use the subject line to organize your e-mails.** When you receive an important e-mail save it to your e-mail files making certain the subject line is clearly labeled showing what the e-mail contains. Change the e-mail subject line if necessary and code it so you know it was changed. You may even want to develop a special code for things using the project name or level of priority and put those codes in the subject line as well.

— Patti Wood

105. **Organize your e-mail files.** Follow the principals of hard file cabinet management on your computer. Keep files of ongoing projects and save only important e-mails to that project file.

— *Patti Wood*

106. **Time your Internet use.** How often do we go to the Internet to look up something and suddenly realize we've been there for hours? Before you begin your research or simply surf the web, set an alarm clock for the maximum length of time you have available for this project. When the alarm goes off, it's time to log off.

— *Martha Lanier*

107. **Everything that happens is either an interruption or a chance to experience WOW.** Which they truly are is generally your choice. Choose to add and experience more WOW in your minutes, hours, days, life.

— Robert Alan Black

108. **Avoid professionals who do not respect your time.** Whether it is your hairstylist, accountant, dentist or others, let them know that you do not appreciate waiting beyond a reasonable time (i.e., 20 minutes) for a pre-arranged appointment. Advise them that an unjustified lengthy wait can cause you to stop using their services.

— Donna Satchell

109. **Isn't it interesting that people will often work harder for free after work than they do at work?** Think about all the volunteer work people do after work, such as Girl or Boy Scout leadership roles, church committee chairpersons, memberships in Rotary, Kiwanis, Optimists, PTA/PTO, involvement as a soccer, little league, basketball, and or football coach. You get the idea. Why? Because when they are involved with these endeavors, *they are somebody!* People look to them for decisions, for direction, for advice. They have status and they are appreciated and respected — things they often don't get at work. Look for ways to tap those natural talents to accomplish more at work.

— *Greg Maciolek*

110. **Post a schedule of your availability outside your door and ask people to sign up for appointments.**

— *Vicki Anderson*

111. **If you find you are torturing yourself by agonizing over a job you need to do but don't feel like doing, either block out the time to jump in and get it done or carve up the overwhelming task into small pieces and do the next logical piece.**

— Diana Grippo

112. **Watch out for the trap of perfection.** The good may be the enemy of the best, but perfection is often the enemy of getting it done at all.

— Mike Monahan

113. Learn to linger. **Piddle and putter for breakthrough, innovative thinking.**

— Edie Raether

114. **Count the cost of *free*.** Don't be deceived by claims of free samples or information. The hidden and exorbitant cost is *your time*.

— John Storm

115. **Use all available resources.** No need to add using pencil, paper, fingers and toes when a calculator is right at your fingertips.

— *Pat Veal*

116. **Use colored dots to assess your time.** If you use a monthly calendar, use colored sticky dots to code your projects. For example, red dots for days that big projects or presentations are due, orange dots on day that you are working out of town, yellow dots for days with long meetings, green dots for personal obligations such as dentist appointments or PTA meetings, and blue dots for fun activities, parties, dates, family time. Now you can look at your calendar and see how you spend your time and where to put new tasks. For a balanced life, make sure you have lots of blue dots.

— *Patti Wood*

117. **Learn *Multiplication BrainStorming*.** Discover how to use more than 25 known *BrainStorming* techniques so you can quickly generate new ideas. Or create your own techniques.

— *John Storm*

118. **Close your door** and you will decrease interruptions. Do not have a door? Hang a sign that says, *genius at work.* When the sign is displayed it is a signal you are deep in work.

— *Doug Smart*

119. **Graduated file stand.** Keep a graduated file stand on the corner of your desk for your high priority projects that need daily attention. This way they are handy, always visible and easily accessible. No more *out of sight, out of mind* problems!

— *Martha Lanier*

120. **You will get a greater sense of accomplishment by daily making a new list of tasks you want to do that day and completing those items.** A running list of projects is defeating to look at because you know it won't get done.

— *Vicki Anderson*

121. My friend and time management guru, Bob Heavers, suggests that you **set up three folders in your office: tasks, projects and reading.** Twice a day, take material coming into your office, and if you determine you must take some action, decide when and make a note in your planner. Then file under tasks, projects or reading as appropriate. PS. File the things you don't have to do in your out box or recycling can.

— *Mike Monahan*

122. **Periodically re-establish control.** Time and priority management is an ongoing process. All but the most disciplined (compulsive) of us will fall behind in managing time and tasks. Just start over whenever necessary. Clean your office and desk, use the 3 holding files system and reprioritize your time. Reestablish use of your planner.

— Mike Monahan

123. Think systems. **Explore everything you do more than once and either discover or create a system for simplifying the actions or steps that you need to take.**

— Robert Alan Black

124. **Organize your files.** Have the major categories of your file drawers listed on the outside of your file drawers.

— Patti Wood

125. **Do it right the first time.**

— Pat Veal

126. **Focus on one task at a time.** You will complete it faster, allowing you to go on to the next important task. All important tasks take time and energy so stay concentrated on one item at a time.

— Linda Edgecombe

127. **Try turning off the radio or stereo when you are trying to accomplish an important task.** Many times the background music can be disruptive instead of being beneficial causing us to spend more time than necessary to finish a project.

— Donna Satchell

128. **Body language is more important than words when communicating with someone.** Your body language, tone of voice and words must be congruent or the message is dismissed.

— Greg Maciolek

129. **Go through your e-mail only once or twice a day.**

— *Vicki Anderson*

130. **When a client calls, call him or her back as soon as possible.**

— *Diana Grippo*

131. **Do business in their office.** Your principle advantage is you can leave. And an advantage to leaving is you can send a clear signal that you place a high value on your time. It might sound like this, in a respectful and firm tone as you head toward the door. "Boss, I'd love to look at pictures of your sister's wedding but you don't have a good audience right now. The Johnson Project that I'm working on — there are some things I want to get finished this morning before 11:00. I'd love to see the pictures. Let's do this later."

— *Doug Smart*

132. **Eliminate tolerations.** Look in your desk drawer, pencil holder or junk drawer in the kitchen and throw away all of the pens that skip, smudge or are out of ink. This way you won't waste time always picking the one that doesn't work.

— Martha Lanier

133. **Good concentration for most people lasts about two hours.** If you are working on a larger project, break it into smaller chunks.

— Linda Edgecombe

134. **Premium intake only, please!** Kick the adrenaline habit by fueling your body with premium fuel instead of the commercialized quick fix. The old axiom "We are what we eat" is still true, so load up on premium fuel.

— Jo Spurrier

135. **It is easier to *replace* a thought, than it is to *block out* a thought.**

— Joe Gandolfo

136. **Use the power of questions.** Asking questions is one of the most effective time-saving techniques known to mankind. Use your inquiring mind to gather input from others.

— John Storm

137. **Time may not be the ultimate measure of efficiency, but rather effectiveness.**

— Edie Raether

138. **It is important to identify those events over which we have no control, but to which we need to adapt by doing whatever it takes to hang in there.**

— Vicki Anderson

139. **When time is short for you, stand when talking on the phone.**

— Robert Alan Black

140. **Whenever possible use technology to perform routine tasks.** Many activities (such as shopping, paying bills, renewing car registrations, etc.) can be accomplished quickly and easily through websites. Find out which ones are safe to use. It can save you many hours that can be put to better use.

— *Donna Satchell*

141. **Minimize *time stealing* by doling out slices of your time.** Offer this to an interrupter with whom you want to speak: "Right now I can talk with you for 4 minutes. What do we need to discuss?" And at the end of four minutes, if the talker has not said something that you feel is worthy of more time, politely end the conversation. If he has, then either agree to extend the conversation or set a time to continue it.

— *Doug Smart*

142. **Have some long term goals, but work from a *90 Day Action Plan*.** Break down your next 90 days into 7 day *just do it activities*. All of the 7 day *just do it activities* work toward accomplishing your *90 Day Action Plan*. This is manageable and it keeps you focused and motivated.

— *Linda Edgecombe*

143. **Plan out your drive so that you complete several errands at one time.** Driving to accomplish only one task can be a waste of time. Bundle tasks together for a productive use of your driving time and gas.

— *Donna Satchell*

144. When a person comes into your office to chat, grab your coffee cup and say, **"I was just on my way to get a cup of coffee, so why don't you join me and tell me as we go?"**

— *Vicki Anderson*

145. **A wise company helps employees satisfy their individual needs at the same time they are satisfying organizational needs.**

— *Greg Maciolek*

146. When you send an e-mail that requires several responses, **put your questions, issues or requests in bullet points.** Ask the receiver to respond inside your e-mail. This saves time, multiple e-mails and creates much fewer misunderstandings.

— *Patti Wood*

147. **Expand your abilities.** Strengthen your strengths and delegate your weaknesses. Why do we often think we have to know a little about everything? Why not take what we do know, increase our knowledge and become expert? We can then delegate what we don't necessarily need to know.

— *Martha Lanier*

148. **Enter follow-up reminders in your planner** of the deadline and check-up dates you want to be reminded. You no longer have to try hard to remember — because you will be reminded automatically on that date.

— Vicki Anderson

149. **If you get lots of phone calls in your day, screen your calls or have your voicemail pick up some.** Let the callers know you will be returning calls at _____ o'clock. They will come to expect your response then, allowing you the time you need to focus on your present task.

— Linda Edgecombe

150. **Get complete information and understanding before starting a project.** No need trying to create a widget if you don't have a concept of what one looks like.

— Pat Veal

151. **Work in blocks of time.** If you have a favorite TV show, you have learned how to block out the world so you can be available at a certain time on a certain day every week. Do the same with an important and routine job you have at work. Just as your family has been trained not to interrupt you during your show, your co-workers will come to realize you have a weekly appointment with your own work that is also inviolable.

— Doug Smart

152. **Great minds discuss ideas.** Average minds discuss events. Small minds discuss people. What do you spend your time discussing?

— Donna Satchell

153. **When you're going to be traveling to see a customer, maximize the value of your trip by calling on other customers or prospects.** It might be a visit or phone call that's as simple as, "Hi ____. I'm working in your city today with ____ and I could not be here without calling to see how I might be of service to you, too."

— *Diana Grippo*

154. **Pre-plan — as much as possible — things like meetings and phone conversations.** Unplanned meetings and conversations often take longer than necessary or expected, and even worse, often do not produce the desired results. Prior to meetings or conversations, jot down your purpose and the desired outcome of the meeting or conversation. Use the same note to record the results of the meeting or conversation and keep in your planner if there is any follow-up. Time activate any to-do's.

— *Mike Monahan*

155. **Use the *business card trick* to save time and stress on your memory.** When you meet someone and get their business card.

• Read the card and make a positive comment about some element to the card giver.

• If you need to take action on the card and cannot make a note on the back, fold the card and tell the person why you are folding it.

• Fold in half to signal the person is a very important contact and you need to be in touch with him in the next few days.

• Top right corner — You need to call or send them something in the next month

• Bottom left corner — You will keep them in your data base

• Your secret — no fold — a card you can toss and not waste time trying to remember if the person was important to you.

—Patti Wood

156. Reverse the question. **Make sure that accomplishing *more* is really what will help you reach your goals.** Remember the story of the man who climbed the ladder faster than anyone else, only to discover that he'd placed his ladder against the wrong wall.

— *John Storm*

157. **Know what you are good at and outsource what you are not good at.** Get help with doing your books, promotional material, cleaning your home, and any other tasks you may not be good at. Spend your precious time doing what you do best. You will accomplish more in less time.

— *Linda Edgecombe*

158. **Know your own productive time.**
Are you a morning, afternoon, evening or night person? As dictated by our Circadian Rhythms, each of us has a time of day in which we are at our creative best and capable of getting more done, quicker. Do work that requires your best, during your best time. Save busywork and less important tasks for your less efficient time.

— *Mike Monahan*

159. **Sort papers, piles and projects by *must be done soon, needs to be done soon, would be nice if done soon* and *others*.**
Focus on the first two and allow yourself to work some on the *nice if done* pile occasionally as a break from the *musts* and *needs*.

— *Robert Alan Black*

160. **Relaxation response techniques will help you get more accomplished.** They will help you progress from a state of stress to a state of calm, which will help you to reverse the negative effects of a tensed body and distracted mind.

— Joe Gandolfo

161. **Follow a plan that is self tailored.** Trying to follow a plan designed for a right-handed person can be frustrating for a left-handed person. Instructions in Spanish are worthless for an English-only speaking individual.

— Pat Veal

162. **Focus on what is meant not what you think was said or you wanted them to say.**

— Robert Alan Black

163. **Create a complete extra set of toiletry items that you use when you travel.** Keep them in your suitcase and do not borrow from it. For women this means a complete extra set of make up. Now you will never have to waste time packing and unpacking all those small items or shopping for something you forgot.

— Patti Wood

164. **Lighten up! Schedule spontaneity!** We tend to try to work more instead of wiser. Take a few moments and gain clarity by giving your mind a mental break. Take time out to lighten up; you will be amazed at the energy boost this will give you.

— Jo Spurrier

165. **Consider hiring others to do tasks for which you are ill equipped** (such as yard work, painting, filing your taxes, etc.). Such tasks can become time-consuming activities that rob you of valuable hours that could be spent on your priority projects.

— Donna Satchell

166. **In order to feel in control, you must understand your real limits of control over the events in your life.**

— Vicki Anderson

167. **Be a coach and not a referee!** Many managers are referees; they mostly speak when people screw up. Coaches help their people learn from their mistakes and coach them to avoid similar mistakes in the future.

— Greg Maciolek

168. When writing, when your mind simultaneously delivers multiple ways to express something, don't take the time to pick the best way. Don't slow down to censor yourself. **If you want to keep in the flow, use/utilize/ make use of slashes so you have all your choices in front of you.** You can decide/edit/delete later.

— Diana Grippo

169. **Place papers in the file folder or drawer that indicates the next action to be taken.**

— Edie Raether

170. **If you enjoy working with others, do difficult tasks with friends or business colleagues.** A team approach can make a difficult project more enjoyable and easier to accomplish. All the parties can benefit because the tasks get done in less time, thus freeing up time to attend to other projects.

— Donna Satchell

171. **Motivation is internal.** Short of a gun or large knife, you can't make anyone do anything they don't want to do. People do things for their reasons not yours, even at work. Find out what are their needs and help provide them the channel to satisfy those needs.

— Greg Maciolek

172. **Beware of what you eat at lunch as it affects your energy levels after lunch.** Avoid high fat, heavy lunches with gravy, rich desserts. Also a liquid lunch (aka, liquor) is very tiring and is certain to make your after lunch productivity almost nil.

— *Linda Edgecombe*

173. **One of the best ways to accomplish more is to spend more time creating solutions and less time dwelling on problems.** Because time is so valuable, don't waste it on trying to change what has already happened. Focus on what can be improved or solved.

— *Martha Lanier*

174. ***The Time Smart System*™ can help you dramatically boost your productivity.**

• **Use the last 15 minutes of your professional day to plan your next day.** It will bring closure to your day, which will help you *leave work at work* so you can relax and enjoy your *other* life.

• **Make a "to do" list and prioritize it.**

• **Daily, schedule your top three priorities.** Most people do not get their number-one priority for the day met, much less their top three. When you consistently focus on accomplishing your top three priorities every day, five days a week, fifty weeks a year, year after year, you are miles ahead of the pack in productivity.

• **Keep a *Great Ideas* file for collecting your flashes of brilliance. until you are ready to act on them.** For example, when you have a great idea on how to improve a project, solve a problem, or enhance a relationship, write it down and drop it into your

Great Ideas file. Then at the end of every day, when you use your last 15 minutes to plan your next day, quickly review your Great Ideas file. Ideas that strike you as *time to act on this* get moved to your to do list.

• **Keep an *Accomplishment* file to record daily what you did that was of particular value.** In the beginning you may have just one or two items worthy of listing although you worked on many things. But even with one or two a day, in a year's time you will have documented 300 to 600 specific examples of your accomplishments. This exercise will help you stay focused on accomplishing the big payoff items in your life, build your self-confidence, and help you document your value in your workplace (which could be a priceless asset at your annual review). Bonus tip: Once you get into the daily groove of identifying your important accomplishments, you will likely record 4 to 8 examples a day, which is as many as 2,400 per year. That's a lot!

— Doug Smart

175. Have a plan, even if it is a rough plan. **Having no plan to work from is like the person who doesn't know the words, trying to sing a song.**

— *Pat Veal*

176. **You will always find time for the critical events.** Make sure those critical events are also important in your life plan.

— *Vicki Anderson*

177. **It is easier to stay focused when you are having fun.** Find fun in what you are doing and/or do what you are doing in fun ways.

— *Robert Alan Black*

178. Be a novice. **Try tackling a task you have never done before.** Besides accomplishing the new task you will accomplish something else — you will grow in your abilities!

— *Diana Grippo*

179. **Cluster your contacts.** Keep your database current so that when you're traveling, you can maximize each trip by knowing all prospects, clients, resource people, associates and friends within the same region.

— *John Storm*

180. **Use drive-time wisely. Listen to audio tapes and CDs which will help you become an expert in your field of endeavor.** You can also listen to programs that can help you manage your time more effectively, motivate you to higher levels of achievement or teach you skills needed to make you more knowledgable of various subjects.

— *Donna Satchell*

181. **Be *present-oriented.*** Frenzy and fretting fragment our focus.

— *Edie Raether*

182. **Slow down to speed up.** Breath, focus on one item at a time, complete it and then move on. By working at high speed, you may look like you are accomplishing a great deal, yet you are most likely spinning your wheels in the same place. This *keep it simple* method allows you to immerse yourself in your task without the distraction of juggling multiple tasks.

— Jo Spurrier

183. **Build your success on the success of others.** Contact people who are already successful in what you want to do and ask them to be your mentor. Most people are flattered you've asked them and are willing to support you and offer guidance. Most of the time all we have to do is simply ask.

— Martha Lanier

184. **Members of a team must participate when setting team goals.** Without participation, there is no ownership. No ownership, no deep commitment to accomplish the group goals.

— Greg Maciolek

185. **Discourage unexpected visitors at home by letting them know you prefer for them to call before stopping by.**

— Donna Satchell

186. **Who is wearing the white hat?** If you are always wearing the white hat and the other guy is always wearing the black hat in a conflict, you are setting yourself up to have a shoot-out . Take off the white hat and ask yourself what you can do to change the situation. It will save you time and aggravation later.

— Patti Wood

187. **Discover your *learning style*.** Are you a visual, aural, kinetic, or other type of learner? Once you discover your style, you'll be able to shorten the amount of time it takes for you to gather useful information.

— John Storm

188. **Know your purpose in every situation.** Before entering any situation, know your intended outcome. By knowing your purpose, you are more likely to achieve it.

— Jo Spurrier

189. **Set up short-term follow-up files to store items related to follow-up actions.** Reference where you put the item by listing the file name in parentheses after the "to do" list reminder you have entered on a future date.

— Vicki Anderson

190. **Nothing is really work unless you would rather be doing something else.**

— *Edie Raether*

191. **Set agendas together beforehand when possible and then review and refine the agendas with realistic time goals at the beginning.** Ask for or assign a timekeeper and revisit your agenda periodically to check how effective you are.

— *Robert Alan Black*

192. **Delight in the perfect present.** 90% of the time, wherever we are, we're not there! In other words, we are not mentally present. At work we spend time thinking about the 'to-do' list at home. Sunday afternoon, we start thinking about the piles on our desk back at work. Be present, wherever you are.

— *Jo Spurrier*

193. To varying degrees, letting go is hard for everyone. But **when you open your hands and let go of something that enables you to receive something.**

— Joe Gandolfo

194. **Signal when you can meet.** When someone interrupts you and you do want to meet with them, but not now, offer a time when you can be available. "Susan, I'm up to my eyeballs in this Johnson Project. How about we meet in the morning at 9? I'll be clear-headed and better able to help you with your budget." You said yes to the interruption but on your schedule.

— Doug Smart

195. **One step at a time.** Break each of your goals into smaller ones, then break them down again. Continue this process until each one is doable.

— Martha Lanier

196. **Know yourself, especially your strengths, weaknesses and passions.** Many people find themselves frustrated because they haven't figured out who they are. Start the adventure of self-discovery and you'll discover how your unique gift mix can help you accomplish your goals.

— John Storm

197. **Adopt, adapt, create — in that order!** All too often we try to do things from scratch when another solution is already available. At the very least, there are usually partial solutions available that would only require some adaptation.

— Mike Monahan

198. Get proper rest. **Fatigue is a time bandit.**

— Pat Veal

199. **Cluster items together.** Make sure if you are going out to run one errand, that you include other things you could readily accomplish while out. Avoid making one-item trips.

— *Linda Edgecombe*

200. **Do not start your day by answering e-mails.** The tasks in the e-mails may not be what is most important. Start your day by reviewing and adding to your prioritized "to do" list.

— *Patti Wood*

201. **To thine own self be true.** If you are a right-brain, divergent, visual, spacial learner, having piles in plain sight fit your organizational style. If you are a left-brain, convergent, linear learner, vertical files and numerical systems will serve you best.

— *Edie Raether*

202. Deep breathing techniques can help reduce your stress —*fast.* **To develop an effective deep breathing technique:**

• Sit quietly for a few minutes each day and take three deep diaphragmic breaths, slowly, through your nose.

• Continue to inhale slowly and deeply, filling your chest completely with air, holding each breath momentarily.

• Breathe as fully as you can without discomfort. Now continue to focus on your breathing and/or refocus when your mind becomes distracted.

— *Joe Gandolfo*

203. **Avoid negative people.** They can drain your energy and prevent you from accomplishing as much as you could have. Whether they are office colleagues, friends or family members, limit your time with them. Negative people can leave you unmotivated to accomplish your tasks.

— Donna Satchell

204. **Be aligned with *why* you are doing each task.** Understanding why you are engaged in a task is paramount to productive work. When the why is clear, the 'what' and 'how to' naturally fall into place.

— Jo Spurrier

205. **Goals must be achievable and measurable and have a written action plan to accomplish them.** Otherwise, goals are just dreams.

— Greg Maciolek

206. **Genius does not succeed alone.** It is well known that Thomas Edison was a genius and a great inventor. He was given 1,092 patents. What many people overlook while praising Edison is that he built his *success team* by employing very intelligent people, including a young Henry Ford, to work in his businesses and dream up new inventions. Edison did not succeed alone.

— *Doug Smart*

207. **Ask the *busy bees*.** Interview the busiest people you know. Ask them how they do it. See what tips they can share that fit with who you are.

— *John Storm*

208. **Know your own energy clock.** Work on tougher tasks when you are sharpest. And less demanding activities when your energy levels are low.

— *Linda Edgecombe*

209. **Consider limiting your multi-tasking to increase your productivity.** Some studies indicate that multi-tasking reduces productivity instead of increasing it. Such research indicates that it may be counterproductive to do certain complex tasks simultaneously. In fact the more complex and complicated the tasks, the greater the chance of lost productivity due to a lack of focus and concentration. Know when to multi-task and when do tasks separately.

— Donna Satchell

(PS: This is a lesson I had to learn!)

210. Time is fair to everyone. No one is discriminated against. **We each get the same 168 hours each week.**

— Joe Gandolfo

211. **Problem free e-mail attachments.** When you are starting a message that will include an attachment follow these steps.

• Type in the person's e-mail address.

• Attach the attachment.

• Open the attachment and check it carefully. Scan it all the way to the bottom of the documents. Make sure it is the correct version of the document.

• Type the e-mail message to the recipient making sure you mention the attached file by name. Request they call or e-mail you confirming they have received it.

• Open your "sent" file to make sure the e-mail with the attachment shows up as sent.

— *Patti Wood*

212. **Simplify, simplify, simplify.** Periodically review your filing system(s) and simplify them. If necessary ask a professional organizer to review your systems and make recommendations for how to improve them.

— Robert Alan Black

213. **On writing projects, you cannot wear your *creativity hat* and your *editing hat* at the same time.** When you are creating a speech, report, proposal, etc., create! Later, go back with a critical eye and edit.

— Diana Grippo

214. **Resist the temptation to stop and look at each item someone puts on your desk at that moment unless they indicate it is urgent.**

— Vicki Anderson

215. **Time is not an external essence, but an internal insight.** Its reality lies in our perception, for one's awareness of time is translated into the body and can kill or preserve us, serve or slay us.

— Edie Raether

216. **Know what feeds your soul and fill it to capacity daily.** Perhaps it is starting each day with a motivational reading, a cup of tea in a quiet corner, or a stroll around the block. A mental diet of daily *soul food* fuels you for the day.

— Jo Spurrier

217. **Experiment with what works best for you.** People thrive in different environments. Find the ones you work in best.

— John Storm

218. **Make commute time productive.** Whether it is 10 minutes or 2 hours, you can dictate notes or letters or listen to tapes and CDs that are beneficial to you.

— *Pat Veal*

219. **Get and stay in good physical shape by exercise and sensible eating habits.** Being in good shape will insure that you have a higher energy level than you would have if you were in bad shape. Higher energy results in the ability to accomplish more.

— *Donna Satchell*

220. Get a quickie. **Use *Quickie Brainstorming* (5 to 10 minute sessions) to rapidly generate multiple solutions and discover new options and opportunities.**

— *John Storm*

221. **Use an organizing system.** The importance of an organizing system cannot be overstated. Whether you use an electronic PDA, a proprietary system such as Priority Management, or a spiral notebook and calendar, keep the following:

- A calendar to record all commitments occurring at a given time and date
- A place to record tasks on the date you intend to do them
- A record of important contacts, meetings and information

— *Mike Monahan*

222. **At times, refuse to allow interruptions.** Become invisible. No calls. No visitors. Ask, "How would this be handled if I were not here?"

— *Pat Veal*

223. **Do you need to shift your time in order to achieve your dreams?** Like everyone else, you have 168 hours in your week. On paper, total the hours per week you spend doing the following: sleeping, eating, driving, working, exercising, spending time with family, playing with kids, watching TV, doing hobbies, and anything else that requires time. Look at where your hours are going. Are you investing your hours in activities that help you achieve your dreams?

— *Joe Gandolfo*

224. Listen to your body. **Take a joy break.** Eliminate time contaminates due to unrelieved stress. Constant work creates an imbalance in your immune system.

— *Edie Raether*

225. **Accept that there are infinite work styles — not just yours.** It is better to accept and understand rather than to continually try to change other people into copies of ourselves.

— Robert Alan Black

226. **Throw things away.** If you're a pack rat, have one day a month, say the last Friday of the month, that is toss-out day. Go through everything and toss generously.

— Patti Wood

227. **Clear you mind as you clear your desk.** As you end an assignment or project, take time to appropriately file all the paper work associated with it. A clean desk and clear mind is much more able to be productive.

— Jo Spurrier

228. **Call ahead if you think you might have to wait.** Whether it is a restaurant, car repair shop or other service provider, find out ahead of time if there is a possibility that you will have to wait before being served or attended to. If the waiting will disrupt your day, plan the activity for later in the week or month.

— *Donna Satchell*

229. It is imperative that all ideas get aired at solution-seeking meetings. **There are no bad ideas when you are trying to solve problems or go in new directions.** If this were so, we would still be riding horses and hunting with knives and arrows.

— *Greg Maciolek*

230. **If you think you don't have time for helping others, such as doing charitable work, because you are too busy being productive, then re-think your definition of productivity.** Adding to corporate revenue is not the only way to be productive. Being a positive role model to someone — whether it be your child or a less experienced colleague is— in the long term, one of the most productive things you can do.

— Diana Grippo

231. **You will accomplish more if you make to-do lists for 60% of your discretionary time because "stuff" will take up the other 40%.** You can always add a few bonus items in case the full 40% doesn't happen.

— Vicki Anderson

232. **If you have no one to delegate to around you, think about what other sources of people there are available: vendors, suppliers, contractors, friends, or relatives.**

— *Robert Alan Black*

233. Practice this formula for increasing your confidence to accomplish more:

Build on your experience
\+ Prepare, prepare, prepare
\+ Focus on the *big picture*
\+ Reject negative self-talk
\+ Trust in your abilities

Greater Confidence and Success

— *Joe Gandolfo*

234. **Time flies when you're having fun because we are, in fact, more productive and efficient with a playful attitude which energizes and motivates.**

— *Edie Raether*

235. **Scheduling your top three priorities every day is smart but does not mean you will get all three completed.** Some days you will barely slog through half of your first priority. Persevere! You will accomplish more by staying focused than by winging it.

— Doug Smart

236. **As you create goals to stretch to, remember that even stretch goals should be reachable.**

— Pat Veal

237. In any situation or moment in your life you have the ability to choose how you respond. You can choose to be negative or positive. **You are in control of your attitude.**

— Joe Gandolfo

238. **When it comes to getting organized around your home, *good enough is just great!*** Leave it at that.

— Linda Edgecombe

239. **Borrow trouble.** Ask your mentors and other people you consider to be successful about the biggest mistakes they've made. Learning from others' mistakes can save you a huge amount of time and painful consequences.

— John Storm

240. **Use your voice mail for messages.** When you have an announcement or need some data from people calling and cannot personally answer the phone, leave a request for the information on your message. For example, "If you are calling to register for the class on Negotiating Skills, please leave your name, department and ID number. I will send you a confirmation." This will save you call-back time in most cases.

— Mike Monahan

241. **Have your employees keep records of their performance.** They should send you e-mails of things they have done that would impact their performance review. Have them code the subject line with their name, the year and the word "Review." When you receive it save it to a matching e-mail folder. Have them copy themselves on the message and keep their own records as well.

— Patti Wood

242. **Get a good night's sleep.** It can help you be more alert and able to accomplish more during the day. Although the amount of sleep required varies from person-to-person, the average is between 7 to 8 hours per night. Are you getting your fair share?

— *Donna Satchell*

243. **Tune into your biorhythms.** Learning about your body's preferences for rest, work, food, and exercise will help you maximize your efforts.

— *John Storm*

244. **Identify your natural *in the zone* time of day versus your *in the lull* time of day.** Listen to the "Wise One Within." Your inner clock will guide your productiveness if you let it!

— *Jo Spurrier*

245. Before starting on anything ask yourself: **How else might this be done? Who else might be able to do this for me and how might I help them in return?**

— *Robert Alan Black*

246. **Don't let time be your jailer.** Know there is enough time for all you really need to accomplish. Don't get sucked into the belief system that because it is 6 a.m. it is time to get up or because it is noon you must be hungry or because it is 10 p.m. you must be sleepy. Simply do what you need to do. Time is a tool to be used for your purposes. Don't let it use you.

— *Jo Spurrier*

247. **Colors are for coding and clustering**. Colors can more quickly be recognized than fine print for ease and access.

— *Edie Raether*

248. ***Lifemotized* — becoming hypnotized by your daily routines.** How many times have you driven your car from work to home — all 2,500 pounds of steel, rubber, glass and fuel — and pulled into your driveway and realized that you really don't remember the drive home? Scary, isn't it? And indicative that change is necessary to *un-numb* your mind.

— *Joe Gandolfo*

249. **No matter where you go, have something to write on and something to write with.** Good ideas arrive when our subconscious mind is ready to forward them to our conscious mind, not when it is convenient to us. Many good ideas, opportunities to get things done better and faster, and our creative best are lost because we have no way of capturing the ideas and little chance of remembering them.

— *Mike Monahan*

250. **Brush and learn.** Buy an automatic toothbrush with a timer (most are two minutes) and while you are brushing your teeth, read poetry quotes or pages from this book that you've taped to the mirror.

— *Patti Wood*

251. **Redefine when enough is enough.** We tend to rework the details that may or may not contribute to the overall quality of our task. If you are unable to determine this point, have a peer or friend take a look. Just make sure you are prepared to accept their determination.

— *Jo Spurrier*

252. **Understand what foods make you sluggish and, therefore, make you accomplish less.** These vary from individual to individual. Know your culprits and avoid them, particularly at low-energy times of the day.

— *Donna Satchell*

253. **Work *from* your goals not *towards* them.** By setting goals that fit your purposes in life you can easily ask yourself whether or not the paper you are holding, the pile you are looking at, or the project you are considering beginning really would be beneficial to you.

— *Robert Alan Black*

254. **Know what works best for you and do it that way.** Develop your own methodology. You need not apologize for adopting an approach that utilizes your forté.

— *Pat Veal*

255. **Keep a log of activities related to a person or project.** This is useful in documenting client, employee, or project issues that arise at later times.

— *Vicki Anderson*

256. **Hire people who are different than you.** If you are a manager, avoid the natural tendency to hire people like yourself. And drop the resistance to avoid people who think or act differently than you. This is the biggest mistake managers make. Most managers make their decision to hire someone in the first five minutes of the interview — hardly enough time to conduct a thorough evaluation of the candidate.

— Greg Maciolek

257. Hire right the fist time. **Hire people who are more skilled than you.** Do what you do best and hire or contract out every other aspect of your business. Yes, that could mean hiring a housekeeper, too.

— Linda Edgecombe

258. **Work from *WOW* and excitement.** Look at the things that need to be done. Think about how might they become WOW things to do or what are WOW ways of doing them. The more WOW, excitement and fun you can put into doing the things you are procrastinating about, the more you will accomplish.

— Robert Alan Black

259. **Plan out your clothes, shoes and accessories the night before.** In the morning you will have one less thing to do and you can start off focused on what you want to achieve that day.

— Donna Satchell

260. **Give timely feedback.** When you give an employee praise, when someone completes an important project on time, or when you notice someone has improved on a skill, tell them right then. Ideally, follow it up with an e-mail. You keep a copy in an e-mail file labeled with the employee's name and year and your request that he or she do the same. When it comes time for employee performance reviews you have your work done. You can also keep records of performance improvement requests and reprimands; do not e-mail them to anyone but yourself! Negative information should only be given face to face.

— *Patti Wood*

261. **Thoughts of doubt and disbelief can keep you from accomplishing what you want because they create an artificial barrier *between* you and what you want.** Ironically, many people suppress their desires in order to avoid disappointment, which is guaranteed to create disappointment.

— Diana Grippo

262. **Avoid the excuse, *I don't have enough time.*** It makes you feel like a powerless victim. The reality is, you have every second of time there is to be had, 24 hours a day, 365 days a year. The difference between people who accomplish a great volume of work and those who accomplish little is not time — it is how the time is divvied up amongst the things that can be done.

— Doug Smart

263. **Post an agenda** of the meeting on the wall with the following headings:

• Agenda item

• What needs to be accomplished, what is the objective (on this item today)

• Time allotted

• Action to be taken after meeting (on this item)

• Person(s) responsible for follow through

Fill out the first three items before the meeting begins and make sure the last two are completed before the meeting ends.

— *Patti Wood*

264. When dealing with a potential risk, ask yourself, *what's good about it?* **Make a list of 4 to 144 benefits and good things about the risk.** Allow them to be funny, strange, weird ideas that cause you to laugh. The more you can laugh about a situation the easier it is to deal with it.

— Robert Alan Black

265. **Schedule a weekly *loose-end afternoon* to handle unfinished business.** Don't let your mind be cluttered with old "to do" items. Clear the way for an efficient work environment.

— Jo Spurrier

266. **First we make our habits and then our habits make us.** Successful people have formed the habit of doing those things unsuccessful people dislike doing and will not do.

— Edie Raether

267. **Don't care about who gets the credit.** So much time can be saved and more can be accomplished if you don't spend your energy on getting credit for a great job done.

— *Linda Edgecombe*

268. ***Do it now!*** Prevent hours lost in searching for information when the action required may have taken seconds.

— *Edie Raether*

269. ***Speakerphone* is up high on the best invention list, right next to sliced bread.** It minimizes agitation while on hold. Technology has made phone contact with a live person virtually impossible. To successfully wade through the menu maze could take 20 minutes. Speakerphone frees hands and ears for other activities.

— *Pat Veal*

270. **Break projects down into individual steps and assign deadlines or dates for action to be taken.** Put these items on the "to do" lists for the individual dates.

— Vicki Anderson

271. **Focused people get more accomplished and they earn respect.**

— Doug Smart

272. **Trick your brain by creating premature false deadlines to avoid the stress of last minute rushing, causing accidents and mistakes.**

— Edie Raether

273. **Eliminate *perpetual jobs*, those that never end, by establishing time frames.** Spend only the allotted time for those type assignments and move on to something else.

— Pat Veal

274. **Send a copy to yourself.** When you send an e-mail, which requires important follow up, blind carbon copy (bcc) yourself on it. Then it shows up in your Inbox, too, and you have a reminder of your "to do."

— Patti Wood

275. Use technology that you understand and **develop a group of technology friends who can help you when you have trouble.**

— Robert Alan Black

276. **You have natural talents for what you are good at accomplishing.** Think back to what you especially liked doing as a child. You are probably good at it now as an adult — or you have a dormant talent waiting to be rediscovered!

— Diana Grippo

277. **Getting more comfortable saying *no* is the best way to take charge of your life and establish your priorities.**

— Edie Raether

278. **Eliminate distractions!** Set aside an afternoon and scan your home or office. Make a list of things that annoy or distract you. The fact that they affect you in this manner means they are pulling energy from you. Increase productivity by reducing them, one by one.

— Jo Spurrier

279. **Remember *Monahan's Law:* All things you do take longer to do than you think they will take, even when you take into consideration *Monahan's Law*.**

— Mike Monahan

280. **Establish a calendar for those tasks that have *invisible* time requirements, such as making flight or other travel arrangements.**

— Edie Raether

281. **Do anything 100 times and you can't help but get good.**

— Doug Smart

282. **Celebrate your failures as well as your successes.** That way you won't be as apt to absent-mindedly repeat them, saving you time down the road.

— Linda Edgecombe

283. **Discover your creativity pathway.** Take a drive, a walk, a trip, a tour, or whatever path leads you to consistently generate new ideas.

— John Storm

284. **Don't get stuck in planning the planning stage.** That is a trap that can lead to *meeting just to meet.* Keep moving into action and to completion.

— *Pat Veal*

285. **TEAM: *Together Each Accomplishes More.*** Nurture your nature to do what you do best and delegate the rest.

— *Edie Raether*

286. **Clear your mind of clutter.** When you first wake up in the morning, take five minutes to write down anything that is muddying up your head. Write in a stream of consciousness any thoughts or feelings that are clogging your brain. This is not a journal or a "to do" list. It's junk. Dump thoughts out on the page the way you dump out the trash. Now your mind is clear and you can accomplish much more in your day.

— *Patti Wood*

287. **Eliminate unnecessary interruptions by *pleading* a deadline and rescheduling the conversation.** Then keep the rescheduled conversation appointment.

— *Vicki Anderson*

288. **Examine how you spend your day.** Identify time-wasters and make changes. For several days write out everything you have to do, including phone calls, errands, and thinking time. Analyze all your activities to see how long it actually takes you to do certain things and how much time is spent in unproductive ways. Then make the necessary changes so you can better utilize your time.

— *Donna Satchell*

289. **Designate a specific time for a specific task.** Nothing ever happens in your life until you create a space (a time) for it to happen.

— *Edie Raether*

290. Nido Qubein, a self-made millionaire told me, **"If you wait until you are in the mood you will accomplish very little."**

— Doug Smart

291. **If your desk does not enable you to work more efficiently, you either have the wrong desk or you're using it incorrectly.**

— Edie Raether

292. **Letting things pile up is like an engraved invitation for stress.** Important things can get buried in junk stuff and mandate a time-consuming item-by-item examination. It is easier to find a needle in a haystack of 10 strands than 3000 strands.

— Pat Veal

293. **You don't have to do everything you are asked to do.**

— Mike Monahan

294. **Keep a record of bill and invoice payments.** Keep a notebook of payments even if you pay bills or invoices by phone or computer and use a program such as Quicken. Have a pocket for each month where you keep any hard copies of bills and invoices. Keep a log on each pocket with columns for name of supplier or vendor, amount, date paid, form of payment (include check number or confirmation number), confirmed as received date and name, and any other important data.

— *Patti Wood*

295. Answer interrupting phone calls with "Hello, this is ____, how may I help you?" **If you truly can help, help. If not suggest who else can.**

— *Robert Alan Black*

296. **The key to managing time is managing the events of your life.**

— Vicki Anderson

297. **Create friendly competition with a co-worker regarding amount of work produced or time of completion.** No need to have a big prize. Most times, bragging rights alone is enough incentive.

— Pat Veal

298. **Consider hiring a personal coach to help you move forward on important goals.** Coaches can be valuable in helping you clarify your goals and coming up with strategies you can use to achieve your objectives. Also you may achieve more because you have someone to whom you are accountable and need to report your progress. For more information, visit websites of coaching organizations and those of personal coaches.

— Donna Satchell

299. **Carry a notebook and small pads *sticky notes* with you at all times.** When things come to mind, write them down on a small note sheet and place them in your notebook. When you complete that task either throw it away or put it in a "I've done with this file."

— *Robert Alan Black*

300. **In order to terminate a meeting with a person who does not appear to know when to leave, simply stand up and move to the door.**

— *Vicki Anderson*

301. **Plan for tomorrow.** Spend the last 15 minutes of your workday finalizing the projects you've been working on and spend a few minutes preparing for the projects for the following day. Leaving with a clear desk will jumpstart your tomorrow.

— *Martha Lanier*

302. **Make your list of *100 Lifetime Goals.***
You can adjust it through the years. The benefit to you is there is a greater chance of reaching your chosen goals, than by reaching them by chance. Also, people live longer when they have a reason to live.

— Martha Lanier

303. **Set deadlines for everything.**

— Vicki Anderson

Contributors

Vicki Anderson

Vicki Anderson works with organizations that want to develop top-notch leadership and communication skills that lead to increased performance and profitability.

Contact information:
Vicki Anderson
Anderson Resources
1925 S. Aster Ave.
Broken Arrow, OK 74012
Phone: (918) 252-1027
E-mail: Vicki@AndersonResources.net
Website: www.AndersonResources.net

Robert Alan Black, Ph.D., CSP

Alan S.P.R.E.A.D.s Cre8ng and Creative Thinking throughout entire organizations from their front doors to their executive floors. He works around the world through consulting, speeches, workshops, training programs, books, articles and his website to help as many people as possible tap into and develop their greatest gift —their creativity.

Contact information:
Robert Alan Black
Cre8ng People, Places & Possibilities
P.O. Box 5805
Athens, GA 30604
Phone: (800) 536-0476, pin 2526
E-mail: Alan@cre8ng.com
Website: www.cre8ng.com

Linda Edgecombe

As the Life Perspective Specialist, Linda works with organizations who want their people to re-energize and re-focus both their work and their relationships. Her programs and publications are as welcome as a deep belly laugh and as profound as a good look in the mirror. The result is energized, change-ready teams, and improved bottom lines.

Contact information:

Linda Edgecombe
Learning Edge Resources Corporation
2102 Bowron St.
Kelowna, British Columbia V1V 2L6 Canada
Phone: (250)868-9601
E-mail: info@LindaEdgecombe.com
Website: www.LindaEdgecombe.com

Joe Gandolfo

Joe coaches and speaks to fathers who want to perform at their best with their children, and increase the odds of having a powerful and positive impact on their children's lives. Joe's programs and presentations are not just for fathers, they also are for wives, children, teachers, CEO's, father's to be, those considering fatherhood — anyone who knows, lives, works or plays with fathers.

Contact information:

Joe Gandolfo, M.A., LPC
Gandolfo Enterprises, Inc.
1000 Johnson Ferry Rd., B-200
Marietta, GA 30068
Phone: (678) 640-0000
E-mail: JGandolfo@mindspring.com
Website: www.JoeGSpeaks.com

Diana Grippo

Diana is the founder and Executive Director of Youth Outreach Media Mentor Program Films, a non-profit organization based in the Bay Area of California. YOMMP provides low-income high school-age students an opportunity to explore filmmaking. Students learn all aspects of production, from interviewing to scriptwriting, from filming to digital editing.

Contact information:

Diana Grippo
YOMMP
24500 Amigos Court
Los Altos, CA 94024
Phone: (650) 917-9654
E-mail: DianaGrippo@yahoo.com
Website: www.yommp.org

Martha Lanier

Martha, president of Ignite Your Potential, Inc., is an energetic and entertaining speaker who enjoys sharing her unrelenting belief that anything is possible when we believe in ourselves and never give up. Throughout her programs she encourages others to stretch their comfort zones and enter into a world of unlimited possibilities. By sharing her life experiences, her audiences learn the value in making choices that will ignite their potential and generate maximum results in both their personal and professional lives.

Contact information:

Martha Lanier
Ignite Your Potential, Inc.
P.O. Box 724075
Atlanta, GA 31139
Phone: (888) 205-6413
E-mail: Martha@MarthaLanier.com
Website: www.MarthaLanier.com

Greg Maciolek

Greg is the President of Integrated Management Resources, Inc. His company focuses on providing insight into an organization's culture, leaders, and people in order to help it provide an environment to excel, for enlightened managers to lead, and its people to self-actualize.

Contact information:

Greg Maciolek
Integrated Management Resources, Inc.
P.O. Box 31933
Knoxville, TN 37930-1933
Phone: (865) 539-3700
E-mail: Greg.Maciolek@imrtn.com
Website: www.IntegratedManagementResources.com

Mike Monahan

Mike is a performance coach who focuses on helping teams and individuals improve performance and tend to the human side of change. Mike has developed a very effective system called Targeted Performance Coaching® in which he helps managers and executives change behaviors or add a set of skills necessary to their continued success.

Contact information:

Mike Monahan
Performance Coach
8505 S. Newcombe Court, Suite A
Littleton, CO 80127
Phone: (303) 948-1587
E-mail: M2HRA@aol.com

Edie Raether, MS, CSP

Edie is an international speaker, trainer, performance coach and author of Why Cats Don't Bark. As a change strategist, Edie's mind-empowering strategies provide the power tools for mastering change from the "insight" out, helping individuals and organizations bridge the gap between knowing and doing to maximize performance and productivity.

Contact information:

Edie Raether
Performance PLUS
4717 Ridge Water Court
Holly Springs, NC 27540
Phone: (919) 557-7900
Fax: (919) 557-7999
E-mail: Edie@Raether.com
Website: www.Raether.com

Donna Satchell

Donna is a workplace strategist, professional speaker, trainer and President of Success! Can Be Yours. She works with companies and employees who want to make their workplace a growing, rewarding and fulfilling experience. She works with individuals who want to lead more successful lives. Donna provides both results-oriented workshops and motivational keynote speeches.

Contact information:

Donna Satchell, President
Success! Can Be Yours, LLC
P.O. Box 870067
Stone Mountain, GA 30087
Phone: (770) 498-0400
E-mail: DSatchell@bellsouth.net
Website: www.DonnaSatchell.com

Doug Smart, CSP

Doug helps people work smarter not harder. Although he works with many types of organizations, his expertise is in helping commissioned salespeople find and profit from their natural selling style. This results in customers who choose to work with them, stay loyal, trust their recommendations, and refer their friends and colleagues.

Contact information:

Doug Smart
Grow Your Sales, LLC
P.O. Box 768024
Roswell, GA 30076
Phone: (770) 587-1050
E-mail: Doug@GrowYourSales.org
Website: www.GrowYourSales.org

Jo Spurrier

Jo is a Transition Strategist, known for her unique approach to goal achievement. Her company, Berkana, works with people and businesses to cut through the chaos and confusion that keeps them from getting what they want . . . what they really want!

Contact information:

Jo Spurrier
Berkana
1650-302 Margaret St., #194
Jacksonville, FL 32204
Phone: (877) 422-4466
E-mail: Jo@BerkanaOnline.com
Website: www.BerkanaOnline.com

John Storm

John is the founder and Chief Idea Catalyst of the BrainStorm Network. BrainStorm Network works with people and organizations who want to think and live outside the box of standard paradigms in order to bring their ideas to life!

Contact information:
John Storm, President
BrainStorm Network, LLC
P.O. Box 720275
Norman, OK 73070-4207
Phone: (405) 321-6262
E-mail: John@BrainstormNetwork.org
Website: www.BrainstormNetwork.org

Pat Veal

As a mom, minister, and Marketing Representative with the Georgia Department of Labor, Pat relates experiences and insights that impact people powerfully. In her job search workshops, Pat helps people identify their true skills. Her teaching translates it into different "languages" for different audiences including corporate, government, religious, spiritual, youth, addicted and others. Pat's practical messages are motivational, inspirational and joyful.

Contact information:
Pat Veal
Phone: (404) 696-7961
E-mail:PVeal1@bellsouth.net

Patti Wood, MA, CSP

Patti is the Body Language Lady. Her body language assessments have appeared on the pages of *UsWeekly*, *YM*, *Cosmopolitan* and *Women First*. Fox News Network has tapped her expertise in live, on-air interviews. Besides personal coaching, Patti is hired to lead seminars on body language, teambuilding, public speaking skills, customer service and how to deal with difficult people.

Contact information:

Patti Wood
Communication Dynamics
2312 Hunting Valley Drive
Decatur, GA 30033
Phone: (404) 371-8228
Fax: (404) 315-9288
E-mail: Patti@PattiWood.net
Website: www.PattiWood.net